FIRST SCIENCE LIBRARY
Water Play

- 18 EASY-TO-FOLLOW EXPERIMENTS FOR LEARNING FUN
- FIND OUT ABOUT RAIN, ICE AND HOW WATER WORKS!

WENDY MADGWICK

ARMADILLO

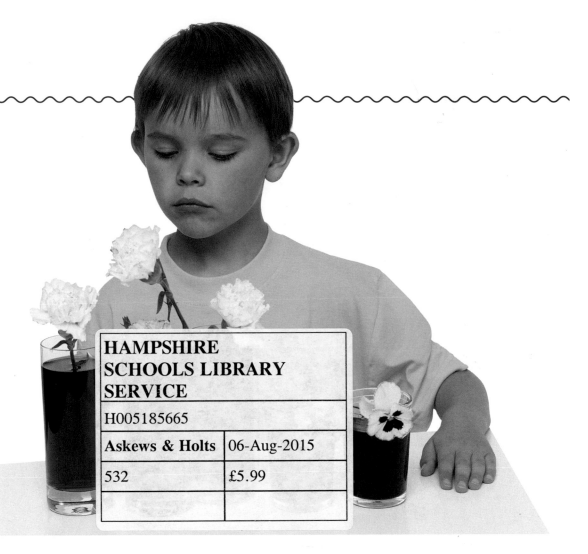

This edition is published by Armadillo, an imprint of Anness Publishing Ltd, 108 Great Russell Street, London WC1B 3NA; info@anness.com

www.annesspublishing.com

If you like the images in this book and would like to investigate using them for publishing, promotions or advertising, then please visit our website www.practicalpictures.com for more information.

Publisher: Joanna Lorenz
Designer: Anita Ruddell
Illustrations: Catherine Ward/ Simon Girling Associates
Photographer: Andrew Sydenham

Many thanks to Ben, Jasmine, John and Poppy for appearing in the book
Additional picture acknowledgements: Sarah Cuttle (page 13 right), Robert Pickett (page 15 top)
Production Controller: Wendy Lawson

PUBLISHER'S NOTE
Although the advice and information in this book are believed to be accurate and true at the time of going to press, neither the authors nor the publisher can accept any legal responsibility or liability for any errors or omissions that may have been made nor for any inaccuracies nor for any loss, harm or injury that comes about from following instructions or advice in this book.

Words that appear in **bold** in the text are explained in the glossary on page 32.

Manufacturer: Anness Publishing Ltd, 108 Great Russell Street, London WC1B 3NA, England
For Product Tracking go to: www.annesspublishing.com/tracking
Batch: 7007-22865-1127

Contents

Looking at water

This book has lots of fun activities to help you find out about water. Here are some simple rules you should follow before doing an activity.

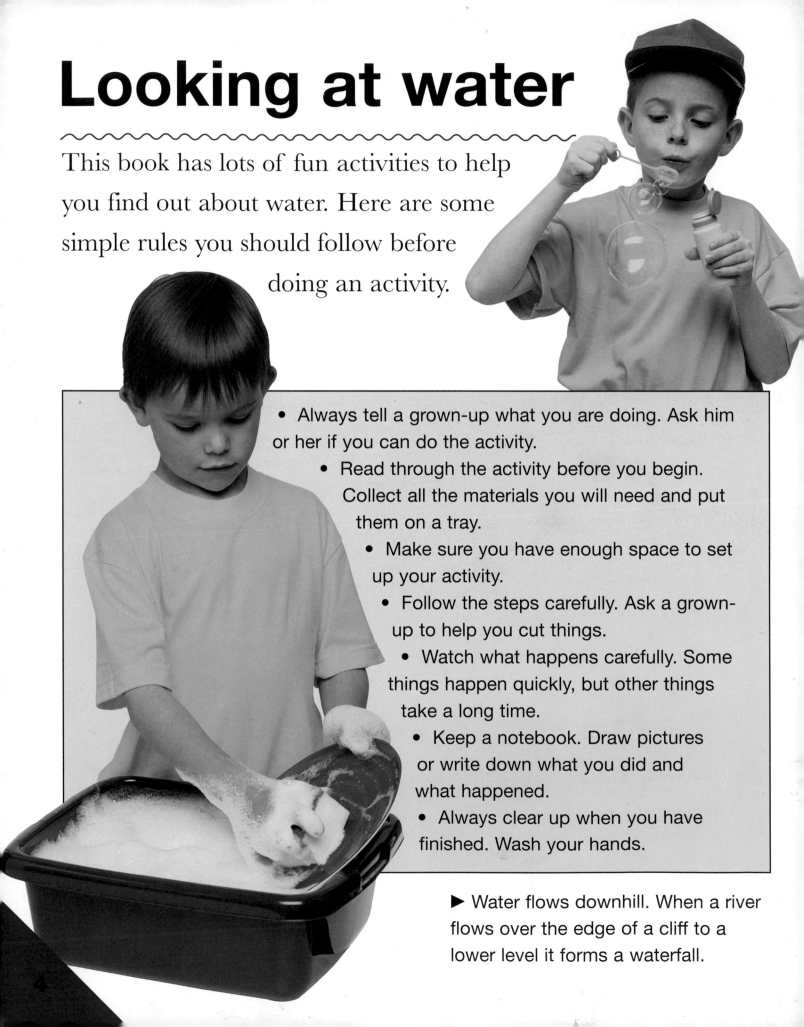

- Always tell a grown-up what you are doing. Ask him or her if you can do the activity.
- Read through the activity before you begin. Collect all the materials you will need and put them on a tray.
- Make sure you have enough space to set up your activity.
- Follow the steps carefully. Ask a grown-up to help you cut things.
- Watch what happens carefully. Some things happen quickly, but other things take a long time.
- Keep a notebook. Draw pictures or write down what you did and what happened.
- Always clear up when you have finished. Wash your hands.

▶ Water flows downhill. When a river flows over the edge of a cliff to a lower level it forms a waterfall.

Wet water

There is more water than dry land on Earth. This water falls from the sky as rain, snow or hail. It collects in rivers and lakes. Water flows downhill until it reaches the sea.

When snow and ice **melt**, they turn into water. That is what is happening to these lumps of ice in Antarctica.

◀ Wet and dry

Is water wet or dry? In this picture four things are wet and four are dry. Can you name them? Make a list of, or draw, some things that are wet.

Catching rain

How much rain falls where you live?
Let's find out.

You will need: empty plastic bottle,
ruler, sticky tape, round-ended scissors.

1 Ask a grown-
up to cut the
top off the
plastic bottle.

4 Put your rain measure outside. Make
sure it is not sheltered from the rain.

2 Use a ruler to mark a scale on a piece
of paper. Tape the paper to the outside
of the bottle.

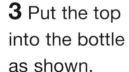

3 Put the top
into the bottle
as shown.

5 Each week look to see how much rain
is in the bottle.

Do not forget to empty it each week.

Stay or go?

Water is a liquid. It can flow and spread out. It can also soak into things. Let's find out what shapes it can make.

Level lines

You will need: empty plastic bottle, cup, water.

1 Pour some water into a bottle. Stand the bottle on a table. Look at the water surface. It is level with the table.

2 Tilt the bottle to one side. Is the water surface still level with the table? Look at the picture to see what happens.

Pour water into a cup or on to the ground outside. See what happens to the water. Describe the shape the water makes each time. Liquids usually take the shape of their containers.

Soak it up

You will need: water, jug (pitcher), saucer, plate, sponge, bowl.

1 Pour some water into a saucer. What happens to it? The water takes the shape of the saucer. The saucer does not soak up the water.

3 Put the sponge on a plate. Gently pour water on to the sponge. What happens to the water? It soaks into the sponge. What happens to the sponge? It feels wet.

2 Now take a dry sponge and squeeze it. Does it feel soft or hard?

4 Squeeze the sponge over a bowl. Water comes out. The sponge has soaked up the water. When you squeeze the sponge, you force out the water.

All gone

Rain makes puddles, but they do not last for long. When the sun shines, the water dries up. We say the water has **evaporated**. Where does the water go?

Quick drying

1 Wet four sheets of kitchen paper.

▲ Why do we hang out clothes to dry? Where do clothes dry best? You will find the answer in this experiment.

2 Lay one piece of kitchen paper in the sun and one in the shade. Hang another on a washing line. Screw one up into a ball. Check them every five minutes. Which one dries first?

You will need: large bowl, water, kitchen paper, washing line, clothes pegs (pins), two drinking glasses, washable felt-tipped pen, clear film (plastic wrap).

Drying out

1 Pour the same amount of water into two glasses. Mark the water levels with a felt-tipped pen. Cover one glass with clear film.

2 Put the glasses in a warm place. Look at them after a few days. Which glass has less water in it?

The uncovered glass has less water. The sun warmed the water. The water turned into droplets called **water vapour**, which went into the air.

Look at the covered glass. Can you see water drops on the underside of the clear film? The water vapour could not escape. It turned back to water on the cool clear film.

Liquid or solid?

Water can be a liquid, solid ice or a **gas** called water vapour. Water vapour is made up of tiny drops of water. You cannot see it, but you can turn it back into water.

Magic water

You can make water appear out of thin air.

1 Pour some cold water into a glass. Put it in the refrigerator for a few hours.

You will need: drinking glass, water, jug (pitcher), small bottle with a narrow neck. You will need to put something in a refrigerator and something in a freezer.

2 Take the glass out and leave it in a warm room. Can you see water droplets on the side of the glass? The water drops have come from water vapour in the air. This vapour cools down on the cold glass. As it cools it forms drops of water. This is called **condensation**.

◄ Look at this photo. The water on this leaf is called **dew**. Where did it come from? (Think about the water on the cold glass on the previous page.)

These leaves are covered with ▶ **frost**. The dew has frozen on them to form frost.

Freeze it

Fill a small bottle with a narrow neck with water. Do not put the lid on. Place the bottle upright in a freezer. Leave it until the water has frozen.

Where is the top of the ice? Is it above or below the top of the bottle? Ice takes up more space than water, so the ice will be above the top.

A magic skin

The top, or surface, of water is special. Drops of water cling together tightly. They make a see-through 'skin'. This is called **surface tension**. Let's find out how we can tell this skin is there.

You will need: tall drinking glass, water, jug (pitcher), dried peas or tiny stones, bowl, round-ended scissors, thick plastic, kitchen paper, metal pin.

Surface view

1 Fill a tall glass to the top with water.

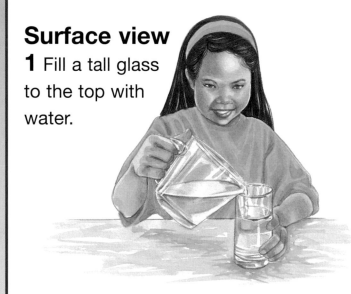

2 Bend down so that your eyes are level with the top of the water.

What shape is the water surface? It should curve downwards in the middle.

3 Drop in a few dried peas or tiny stones. Does the water overflow?

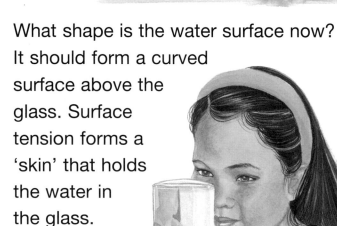

What shape is the water surface now? It should form a curved surface above the glass. Surface tension forms a 'skin' that holds the water in the glass.

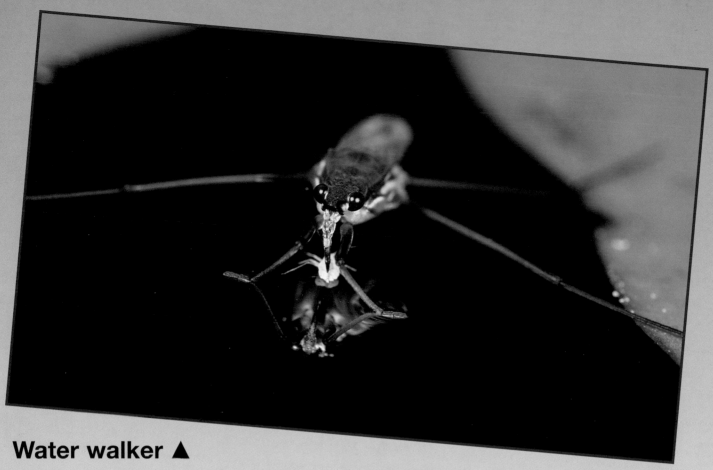

Water walker ▲

This is a pond skater. It can walk on water. Can you see the dents its front feet are making in the water's skin?

A solid surface

1 Fill a bowl with water.

2 Cut a small piece of thick plastic. Carefully put the plastic on top of the water. What happens? The plastic floats on the water.

3 Tear off a small piece of kitchen paper. Put a metal pin on top of it. Float the paper and pin on the water.

See what happens to the pin and paper.

The paper will sink, leaving the pin floating on the surface.

Bubble power

We can change the surface skin of water. We can even make it stretchy. This stretchy skin lets us have some fun. We can blow bubbles. All we need is a soapy liquid.

Bright bubbles

Look at these bubbles. What is inside a bubble? What is around the outside of the bubble?

A bubble is a ball of air enclosed in a stretchy, liquid skin.

Mixing bubbles

You will need: mug, warm water, teaspoon, dishwashing liquid.

1 To make bubble mix, half-fill a mug with warm water.

2 Add about three teaspoonfuls of dishwashing liquid. Mix well.

Blowing bubbles

You can make a bubble blower from a piece of plastic-covered wire.

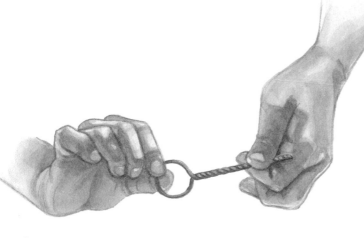

2 Blow gently. What shape are the bubbles you make?

1 Bend one end of the wire into a circle. Leave some wire at the end of the circle. Twist the two ends together to make the handle. Dip your bubble blower into the mix.

Are bubbles always the same shape? Make a square blower. What shape are the bubbles? Now try other shapes. What did you find out about the shape of bubbles? Bubbles are always round.

Waves and currents

Water rarely stays still. Even on a calm day, you will see ripples on the surface of large bodies of water. Waves move over the ocean's surface. They are driven mainly by the wind. Waves usually only affect the surface of the water. At a very deep level in some oceans, the water does move in giant streams called ocean currents.

These can be hot or cold, and can affect the world's climate. Ocean currents are usually caused by differences in the water's saltiness or temperature, rather than by the wind.

Powerful seas

In stormy weather, giant waves rear up and crash down, turning the sea into a raging turmoil.

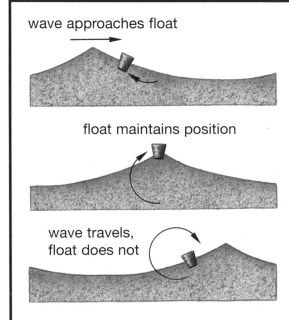

wave approaches float

float maintains position

wave travels, float does not

Wave goodbye

As waves travel across the water's surface, the water itself does not move. The wave passes through the water, while any objects floating on the water hardly move at all.

Making waves

You will need: rectangular plastic bowl, water, bathtub or inflatable pool, non-hardening clay.

1 Place the plastic bowl on the floor or on a table. Choose a place where it does not matter if a little water spills over. Fill the bowl with water almost to the brim.

2 Blow very gently over the surface of the water. You will see that the water begins to ripple where you blow on it. This is how ocean waves are formed by air movement.

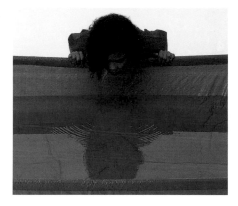

3 Fill the bathtub or pool with water. Blow gently along the length of the bath or pool. Blow at the same strength as in step 2, and from the same height above the water.

4 Keep on blowing for a minute or so. Notice that the waves are bigger in the bathtub or pool, even though you are not blowing harder. This is because they reach farther across the water.

5 Now drop a small piece of clay into the water. Watch how it sets up waves. Ripples travel out in circles from where the clay entered the water.

Going up!

Water usually flows downhill.

However, it can also go upwards.

Water flows up plant stems.

Tinted tubes

You will need: small stick of celery, drinking glass, water, red food dye.

Stand the celery in some red-tinted water. Leave it for a few hours. Cut the end off the celery. Look at it. Can you see the tubes that carry the water up the stem? They should be tinted red.

Fancy flowers

You will need: fresh pale flowers, round-ended scissors, two drinking glasses, water, red and blue food dye. Use very pale flowers. White carnations would work well.

1 Cut off the bottom of the flower stem. Carefully cut up the middle of the stem.

2 Half-fill two glasses with water. Add a few drops of red food dye to one glass. Add blue food dye to the other glass.

3 Put one half of the flower stem into the blue water. Put the other half into the red water.

4 Leave the flower in a warm room for a few hours. What happens to it?

Can you see that some petals have red streaks and others have blue streaks? The flower took up the dyed water through its stem.

These flowers have blue, green and red streaked petals.

Papercraft

Paper is made up of lots of **fibres**. In between these are tiny, tube-like holes. Water will slowly rise up the paper through these holes. We call this **capillarity**.

Water lily

You will need: non-shiny paper, round-ended scissors, large bowl, water.

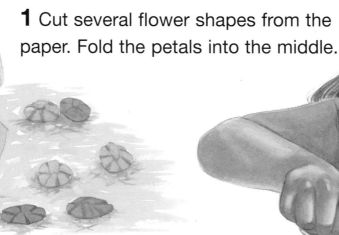

1 Cut several flower shapes from the paper. Fold the petals into the middle.

2 Put some of the flowers in a bowl of water. What happens to the petals? The petals will open as the paper **absorbs** the water.

Incredible inks

We can use water movement through paper to find out which shades make up orange.

You will need: blotting paper, round-ended scissors, washable felt-tipped pens, sticky tape, pencil, empty plastic bottle, water.

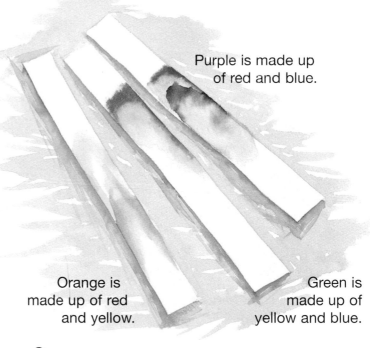

1 Cut a long, thin strip of blotting paper. Using an orange felt-tip, draw a thick band near one end. Tape the other end to a pencil.

2 Ask an adult to cut the top off a small plastic bottle. Put a little water in the bottle. Balance the pencil across the top so that the end of the paper strip is in the water. The orange band must not touch the water. Leave for about an hour.

Purple is made up of red and blue.

Orange is made up of red and yellow.

Green is made up of yellow and blue.

3 Take the paper out of the water and let it dry. The ink has moved up the paper. The orange band has separated into red and yellow. Repeat steps 1 to 3 using a green pen or a purple pen.

Let's mix it

Some solids seem to disappear when you stir them into water. We say they **dissolve**. Some liquids mix with water but others do not.

Mixing liquids

You will need: drinking glass, water, orange squash, jar with lid, cooking oil.

1 Part-fill a glass with water. Add orange squash. What happens? The water and squash mix.

2 Put some water in a jar. Add cooking oil. Put on the lid and shake. Leave the jar to stand. What happens? The oil and water do not mix. The oil floats to the top.

◄ We use detergent to clean greasy dishes. The soapy water breaks up the grease into tiny drops. These float off the dishes and hang in the water, making it look cloudy.

Dissolve or not?

You will need: cold and warm water, drinking glass, washable felt-tipped pen, teaspoon, sugar.

1 Pour some cold water into a glass. Mark the water level with a felt-tipped pen. Stir a spoonful of sugar into the water. It will dissolve. When things dissolve they do not take up more space. The water will stay at the same level.

2 Add another spoonful of sugar and stir again. Does the sugar disappear this time? Keep adding sugar. How many spoonfuls can you add before sugar stays at the bottom?

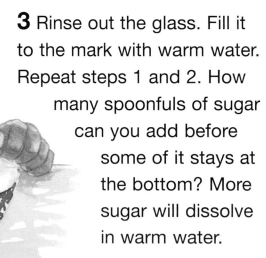

3 Rinse out the glass. Fill it to the mark with warm water. Repeat steps 1 and 2. How many spoonfuls of sugar can you add before some of it stays at the bottom? More sugar will dissolve in warm water.

Water support

Some objects **sink** and others **float** in water. When an object is put into water, it pushes down on the water. The water pushes back. This is called **upthrust**. Which things float and which things sink?

You will need: small objects to put in water.

SINK	FLOAT
stone	feather

Put some objects in a bowl of water, one at a time. Make a list, or draw pictures, to show which objects float and which sink.

Sink it!

Can you make a sinker float? Can you make a floater sink? Let's try.
You will need: large bowl, water, small plastic box with a lid, toy wooden bricks.

1 Half-fill a bowl with water. Fill a small plastic box with water and put its lid on. Put the box into the bowl. Does the box float or sink?

2 Take the box out of the bowl. Empty the water out of the box. Put the lid back on. Does the box float?

3 Take the lid off the box. Does the box still float?

4 Put some toy bricks in the box. What happens to the box? How many bricks can you add before the box sinks?

An object sinks when the upthrust of the water is not strong enough to support it.

Liquid layers

Liquids can float and sink too. It depends on their **density**. Dense liquids are heavy. They will sink in a less dense liquid.

Liquid sandwich

You will need: tall drinking glass, syrup, cooking oil, water, green food dye, jug (pitcher), cork, frozen pea, plastic brick, coin.

1 Pour some syrup into a tall glass. Gently pour on some oil. Does the oil float or sink? It will float.

2 Add some green food dye to cold water. Slowly pour it into the glass. Does it float or sink? The water will settle between the oil and the syrup.

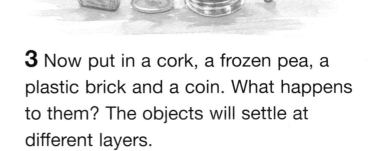

3 Now put in a cork, a frozen pea, a plastic brick and a coin. What happens to them? The objects will settle at different layers.

Marbling

We can use floating oil paints to make pretty patterns. You can make your own.

You will need: oil paints or red and blue powder paint, clean yogurt pot, cooking oil, stick, old dishwashing bowl, water, newspaper, thick paper.

1 To make oil paints, put red powder paint into a clean yogurt pot. Add a little cooking oil and mix. Make blue oil paint in the same way.

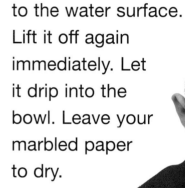

2 Half-fill an old dishwashing bowl with water. Put it on newspaper.

3 Put a few drops of red and blue paint on to the water. Mix them with a stick.

Handy hint: if the oil paint is very thick, it may sink. It this happens, try using warm water in the bowl.

4 Gently lay a piece of thick paper on to the water surface. Lift it off again immediately. Let it drip into the bowl. Leave your marbled paper to dry.

29

Hints to helpers

Pages 6 and 7

Discuss how water flows downhill. Gravity and the contour of the land will determine the speed at which water flows downhill. All water on Earth settles at the lowest level that it can reach.

Discuss the best place to put the rain measure. Keep it out of the wind. Fix the measure firmly in the ground. Suggest that you keep a chart of how much rain falls each week.

Pages 8 and 9

Discuss the fact that the surface of liquids in containers always stays horizontal even when the container is tipped.

Water will soak into some things and not others. Try pouring water on different fabrics. Pour water on chalk, sand and soil. Discuss how some rocks soak up water while others do not.

Pages 10 and 11

Water evaporates most quickly in a warm sunny place. Wind carries away the water vapour that evaporates from the surface of the cloth. This helps the cloth to dry. Spreading out the cloth also helps the cloth to dry as water can evaporate from the whole surface. Therefore, the best drying conditions are warm, windy weather with the clothes spread out.

The heat from the sun makes the water in both glasses evaporate. But the film stops the water vapour from escaping into the air. The water vapour condenses on the film. Water drips back into the glass so that the level of the water stays higher in the covered glass. Discuss the water cycle and how evaporation and condensation work in nature.

Pages 12 and 13

The cold glass cools the air around it. Cool air cannot hold as much water as warm air, so some of the water vapour in the air condenses on the sides of the glass. Discuss where else you can see condensation, e.g. on the inside of windows on cold days or on a mirror in a steamy bathroom. At night the air gets cooler and can hold less water vapour. The water vapour condenses on the cold surfaces of things such as plants. In the winter, the condensed water freezes and the ice particles form frost.

When water freezes it expands. Ice takes up more space than water. Discuss why water pipes sometimes burst in winter.

Page 15

The kitchen paper will absorb water and should sink. If it doesn't, you can gently push the wet paper down at one corner. The pin is left floating on the surface film. If you look carefully you can see the 'skin' bending beneath the pin.

Page 17

A better bubble mixture can be made by adding a few drops of glycerine.

Bubbles are always round in shape because surface tension

pulls the surface of the liquid into the smallest area. For a drop of water, the smallest possible area is a sphere.

Pages 20 and 21

Water travels up the flower through very narrow tubes in its stem by capillary action. These tubes should be seen clearly in the celery stem. The pull of this capillary action is enough to overcome the downward pulling force of gravity. In plants, the loss of water from the surface of petals and leaves (transpiration) also helps to pull the water up the tubes.

Pages 22 and 23

The paper flowers open because the paper absorbs water. As the water rises through the paper fibres, the paper swells up and the petals open.

The felt-tipped pens must be water soluble. The dyes in the pens dissolve in the water. The dissolved dyes move up the paper at different speeds. The different colours in the mixture separate as the water rises through the paper by capillarity.

Page 25

A certain volume of liquid can only dissolve a certain amount of solid. When no more solid will dissolve, a saturated solution is formed. The amount of solid that can dissolve depends on the temperature of the liquid. Warm liquids dissolve more solid than cold liquids.

Try a further test to see which things dissolve and which don't. Try peas, rice and gelatine cubes. You will find that the peas and rice do not dissolve in water. The gelatine will only dissolve in warm water.

Pages 26 and 27

Objects that are heavy for their size will sink. Those that are light for their size will float. You can show this very easily. Put a large ball of non-hardening clay into water. It will sink because it is dense and the upthrust of the water cannot support it. Now flatten the clay into a boat shape with a large surface area. The boat will float. Try other shapes to see which float.

The box full of water may float low in the water or it may sink. If the amount of water displaced by the box weighs more than the box, the box will float. If the displaced water weighs less than the box, the box will sink. The empty box will float higher in the water than the box full of water. As bricks are added the upthrust of the water cannot support the box and it sinks.

Pages 28 and 29

The oil is the least dense liquid and will float on the water. The water is more dense than the oil but less dense than the syrup, so it floats on the syrup.

The objects also have different densities. The coin is very dense and so will sink to the bottom. The cork has a low density and will float on the oil. The plastic brick will probably sink in the oil and float on the water. A large frozen pea will sink in the water and float on the syrup. If the pea is very small, its large surface area relative to its size may cause it to float on the water.

Much better results are achieved with household oil paints. Made-up oil paints must be very well mixed. The oil paints float on the water so you can lift them off with the paper. You can clean the water by placing kitchen paper on the surface.

Glossary

Absorbs Soaks up liquids such as water.

Capillarity The rise of liquids such as water up a thin tube. Surface tension pulls the surface of a liquid up into narrow tubes.

Condensation The tiny drops of water that form on cold things. Water vapour cools down when it touches something cold. It turns into tiny droplets of water that join together to form larger drops of water.

Density The amount of weight an object has for its size.

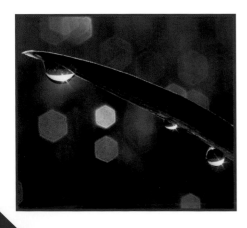

Dew Water drops that form when water vapour in the air cools on cold surfaces. Dew often forms on plants at night.

Dissolve When some things are added to a liquid and they mix completely with the liquid so they cannot be seen.

Evaporated Changed from a liquid or solid into a vapour or gas. Water changes into water vapour which rises into the air.

Fibres Long, fine threads.

Float To stay on the surface of water or another liquid.

Frost Frozen dew, ice that forms on objects outdoors at night.

Gas A substance that has no fixed shape. The tiny bits that make up a gas are spaced so far apart from each other that they are not held together.

Melt When something changes from a solid into a liquid. For example, when you warm ice, it melts into water. Some metals melt when you heat them.

Sink To drop down into water or another liquid.

Surface tension The stretchy 'skin' on the surface of a liquid such as water. This skin is caused by the tiny drops of liquid clinging together very tightly at the surface.

Upthrust An upward push.

Water vapour Very tiny droplets of water in the air. They are too small for you to see but can condense on the surface of a cold object.